feast gently

Other books by G.C. Waldrep

POETRY

Goldbeater's Skin
The Batteries
One Way No Exit
Disclamor
Archicembalo
Your Father on the Train of Ghosts (collaboration with John Gallaher)
Szent László Hotel
Susquehanna
Testament

ANTHOLOGIES

Homage to Paul Celan (co-editor, with Ilya Kaminsky)
The Arcadia Project: North American Postmodern Pastoral
(co-editor, with Joshua Corey)

HISTORY

Southern Workers and the Search for Community

G.C. Waldrep
feast gently

Tupelo Press
North Adams, Massachusetts

Library of Congress Cataloging-in-Publication Data
Names: Waldrep, G.C. (George Calvin), 1968- author.
Title: Feast gently / G.C. Waldrep.
Description: First edition. | North Adams, Massachusetts : Tupelo Press, 2018.
Identifiers: LCCN 2018013985 | ISBN 9781946482112 (pbk. original : alk. paper)
Subjects: | LCGFT: Poetry.
Classification: LCC PS3623.A358 A6 2018 | DDC 811/.6--dc23

Cover and text designed and composed in New Caledonia and Copperplate by Bill Kuch.
Cover: "Shredded," by Richard Cofrancesco. Used with permission of the photographer.
richco@vermontel.net / http://www.racfocus.com.
First edition: May 2018.

Tupelo Press
P.O. Box 1767, North Adams, Massachusetts 01247
(413) 664–9611 / editor@tupelopress.org / www.tupelopress.org

Tupelo Press is an award-winning independent literary press that publishes fine fiction,
nonfiction, and poetry in books that are a joy to hold as well as read. Tupelo Press is a
registered 501I(3) nonprofit organization, and we rely on public support to carry out
our mission of publishing extraordinary work that may be outside the realm of the large
commercial publishers. Financial donations are welcome and are tax deductible.

ART WORKS.
arts.gov
Produced with support from
the National Endowment for the Arts

garments of skin: the phrase gave rise to a great deal of speculation, and a number of very different explanations were put forward, notably:

1. The Hebrew word was read as *'wr,* "light," instead of *'wr,* "skin," and the verse was taken to refer to the pre-Fall state (i.e. "God has made"). This is found in some early Jewish texts and it is the common source of the phrases "robe of light/glory," so common in Syriac writers . . . A variant on this interpretation, found in the Jewish Targums, takes the "garments of glory" to refer to Adam's priestly garments which he took from Paradise.

2. The garments were indeed of animal skin (a possibility which Ephrem envisages), but the implication that an animal had previously been killed led some to suppose that:

3. the "skin" was in fact the bark from trees. This view was adopted by many later Syriac writers, basing themselves on Theodore of Mopsuestia.

4. The "garments of skin" were taken by some (notably Origen) to refer to the human body, implying that the pre-Fall body had been of a different order.

—Sebastian Brock, "Notes to Section II of the
Commentary on Genesis" from
St. Ephrem the Syrian: Hymns on Paradise

Contents

He tested the little pears.

—Geoffrey Hill, from *Mercian Hymns*

feast gently

Their Faces Shall Be as Flames

That was the spring the bees disappeared, we didn't know

where they went, where they'd gone, where they were going, it was a

rapture of the bees, only the weak, the young, the freshly dead

left behind, *a rapture of bees*, my neighbor with the ducks had begun to walk

like a duck, *Follow follow follow Sam* he sang as he walked, and they followed,

· it was that simple, of course I thought of the Piper, although

this procession was more benign, my neighbor's I mean, though he intended

to have each for dinner, eventually, and he did not name them,

as we don't name bees, because we don't see clearly enough

to distinguish them as persons, *person* in the grammatical sense, first second

or third, which is why we refer to them in the collective, usually,

they breed, they swarm, they milk their honey for us

in the collective, and they vanish collectively, is this then the true

rapture, was the one true God after all a god of bees, and now she is taking

them home, is this any more comforting than all the other proposed explanations,

pesticide, fungus, mites, electromagnetism, even the infrasound the giant

windmills make, that sends the bats and raptors

to their deaths, all invention gone awry, hive after hive

suddenly empty, as if they'd all flown out less than purposefully, casually,

and somehow forgotten to come back, held up at the doctor's or the U-Haul

dealer's, swarms of them, hundreds, thousands vagabond

in some other landscape, or rising, *we shall meet them in the air,*

at the post office to mail a letter to a woman who might or might not be my love because a rate change had caught me with insufficient postage

I had to wait, the clerk was preoccupied with a sort of crate

made of wire mesh, through which I could see bees, *Resistant* the clerk said

as she filled out the forms and sent them, registered parcel post, somewhere

else, only then did she sell me the stamp I needed,

or thought I needed, or hoped to need (there is a season

when one hopes to need), and I thought about what it would be like

to mail a crate of bees, *Resistant*, to my love, if I had a love, and have them

vanish en route, the mesh crate arriving dusty, empty, one or two

broken, desiccated bodies rattling lightly around inside, like seeds in a gourd,

or like a child you'll never have, that is, the possibility of that child, the rattling

blood of it, a different sort of vanishing, we would all like to believe

in the act, that Houdini was a man, only a man, as he proved in the moment

and by the precise circumstance of his death, and the fact of his body,

lifeless but extant, rattling around the arcade, the park, the amusement pier

of disturbing coincidences, while in Missouri another hobbyist beekeeper

walks out to her tomblike hives on a spring morning

to find nothing there, just boxes, empty boxes, a sort of game

a child might invent, this rapture, same sort of funny story

a child *will* invent, when shown a photograph, *This is the policeman,*

and this is the woman with two heads, and this, which looks like a modest

red house in a suburb, this is really the ghost of the bees,

a small ghost, a modest ghost, like the ghosts of the locusts and the elms,

not a ghost to trouble us, until (in the photograph) the house spreads its wings

and vanishes, as houses do, or as houses will when the rapture extends

to architecture, the god of small houses having, first, existed, and then wed

the bee god, so that we are left sleeping alone again, and out of doors, in spring, as one more source of sweetness is subtracted from this world

and added to another, perhaps, as we would like to think, one of the

more comforting ideas, a sort of economics, a grand

accounting, until what angel of houses or of bees blows what trumpet,

and we fall as mountains upon the insects, devour them as seas,

scorch the houses as with fire, *we* become the ground that hollows beneath

them and the air they fly through, their wormwood star, as all the bees of heaven

watch from heaven and all the houses of heaven lean down

for a closer look, and the smoke drifts upward, and we are the smoke, we are

only the smoke, inside of which my neighbor walks, with his ducks, and sings,

and they follow, and my hive lazes, drowses as if they or it were dreaming

us, as if they or us were touchable, simple as a story, an explanation,

any fiction, as if they thought of us, or were praying, or were dancing,

or were lonely, as if they could be, or would be, touched.

Like a Fire from Which Sparks Emitted Do Fly Upward

Shocked from sleep in the midst of storm I think *antler-candling*. At first there is no image, only the words against the dulled retinas of the mind's ear at waking, words smaller than lightning but only slightly more permanent.

The storm passes to the south. I hear, from the highway, traffic headed that way. A gunning of engines and blaring of horns.

Sixty-four squares on a chessboard, white on black (or black on white, if you prefer). When I was quite small I imagined the dark squares were deep water, could not understand how the carved tokens floated. I would place the pieces on the board, watch them, remove them. Repeat the process.

To wake with a fragment of language in mind—on the mind's tongue, in the mind's ear—is like trying to remember how a once-favorite pop song went. You ask your friends, but they can't tell you. You try Google. You're aware that nostalgia is an engine of depletion but you keep trying anyway.

Language and image flow through lyric space in parallel streams, like matter and angels from the pedicles of some lesser god. Sleep locks this knowledge into us and swallows the key.

Meanwhile, other songs are being composed, sung, other poems written. Other storms imagined, experienced, weathered.

I don't know whether antler-candling is about deer or about illness or about exogamy, about folk ritual or petty entrepreneurs. Poetry takes language's idea of ornament and replaces it with a beating heart, not knowing sleep stole the heart from some other dreamer.

Jeffers dreamed of deer because, like images, they were the most fragile creatures he could never possess, domesticate, disciple. Their panic-numbed souls carom against the thin walls their bodies make.

Sleep walks down the dark street where language left him, whistling, hands in pockets. Maybe he's got a razor. Sleep is the bruiser language's father warned her about.

In the fields south of town the locals are erecting a temple to the storm. Through the pelting of the rain I hear their ecstatic cries, see the arc of the sodium lights. They press language and image into the service of their worship.

Something is always falling from the sky. A man, a stone, an electrical discharge. A satellite, radiation. Rain. Scientists inspect these apparitions for signs of language.

The faster the film runs, the more secure the illusion. Grammar and syntax are to language what Zeno's paradox is to distance, what electromagnetism is to deer. A shortcut, a shorthand. A useful way of approximating for X.

In the dark, punctuated by flashes of lightning, the antlers of the mind's deer glow, kindle, burn. The eyes of these deer are blank. They all stare toward the dreamer, toward the dream's fragmenting locus in the living circle.

The chaos of the night sky comes to us in the person of something half-man, half-stag. We adjust the object of the hunt's pursuit to suit our various needs. Whole nations pass, whole kingdoms. The huntsman's blink stabs the retinas.

Chess is a system in which some men drown. (Fewer women.) The board hypnotizes the same way a thaumatrope whirls in sunlight, the here and the not-here, a phantom engine. Chess offers a protocol in the absence of deer, of word, of storm.

Language and image, delivered from the clutches of their worshipers, crouch inside the body's darkness. They want to set fire to the tabernacle, inside of which the locals continue to beat their tambourines. Sleep has lent them his cigarette lighter, but they can't seem to get it working properly.

In the forest improvised by sleep the deer run ahead of the storm, antlers aflame. It is impossible for the eye not to follow them, in the same way that it is nearly impossible not to watch a film when it is projected on a screen in a darkened room.

In mythologies as in dreams, stars talk to themselves in the night sky once a storm has passed. They gossip, calculate, plan extravagant vacations. They are too big for sleep to swallow, so he stands just outside their line of sight, on the porch, smoking. Listening.

Jeffers imprisoned himself in a tower so as to be capable of love. He played chess in his dreams, endless matches. Upon waking he could never remember his opponent's face.

In a director's cut, cinematography almost always triumphs over narrative. The long tracking shots; the single eye, lidless, pulsing in the arsonist's slick palm.

To fall back into sleep after a storm is to fall back into the blinded souls deer leave behind, purified and bright, empty of everything save terror and motion. The locals straggle home, their coats and faces blackened.

Latria vs. *dulia:* language *vs.* image, image *vs.* word.

The logic of the deposition is the logic of the witness, vertical. To take down, to render. Something is always falling from the sky. Some Bethel is always burning.

Fox-Breath

(para-chantry)

It would be rank. It would be
mute, & then immutable.
You would not be able to hide
inside it. No language
but misprision, the concept of.
The squalor of it, a poverty
of music unstrung
from the body of intention
with a sailor's knife,
the blade of it a cheek against
some other, crystal cheek.
And you would long
for it, to be delivered from it.
It would not harm you—
not on its own terms,
for its own muscular sake.
You would be as a spirit to it,
an object of devotion.
Feel it caress your flank, the
thin tissues of flesh garlanding
your throat. While you lie
prone in a forest glade.
Your condition is irrelevant
the way the sky, suspended
above the dew-struck
canopy, is irrelevant: a pure
song, a dropped stitch.
The thread entering & then
leaving your body, gold needle
tightening in the dream's
grasp. You would die for this,
is what you are thinking—
Quisling, Magdalene, lictor—
wanting to draw
that close to some living well.

To the Embalmers

in mem. Mahmoud Darwish

I went into the desert for the velvet flesh of two white fish.
And when the heat of the desert was withdrawn from me
I settled my chair by my heart's black flame. A shepherd
taught me the echo of the stars' exquisite math which sounds
in the night like a mesquite blossom. Small and golden

I approached the bridge I had left inside the unfinished book
where my faith lay dammed. Dip your finger in the rods
and cones of the desert's perfect eye, all who could not die
were singing up to me. There is no "final rose," I replied,
only a succession of beds on which the clouds take their blue

rest. In the arroyos a trickle of honey gathered in search
of the bees that had chained it to a prayer. I gazed into it
and saw my name spelled again in the worn boards
of a pine floor, a stitched cloth over which the brass gears
of my father's war presided. My father went into the desert

for a new flag to drape over the sleeping body of my mother,
who had rubbed salt and cumin into the twin clefs
of her neck and shoulders after she, impoverished, received
the emperor's summons. Now I ask the moon to testify
to my body's chill, the unaccompanied music that bandages

the return of the dead. I have no patience and the almond
cake is bitter on my tongue. What am I to call you
when I see you freshly clothed in the catenaries of swallows?
I who *chose* exile from the land's sleep-script, its strange
harvest borne upward by a wind from deep inside the earth.

If I go there now I will find another poet in my house
from which my Christ has wandered, a shadow falling clean

across the sea's torn hem. I will follow Him into the smallest
wilderness. There is no Babylon like the soul's Babylon,
its hanging garden wreathed in the voices of created things.

Strike the pen from my hand if I have misunderstood how
the dust returns to us, through the smallest dances.
In the coasts of my adoption I grow colder, I cross my chest
with a map of all the sun has denied. The temples lie
behind me now as the bodies of women. Breathe on me,

my childhood in the lost city of love. Let me be the only
casualty, the waking wound towards which the forest
of my fading heat is climbing. This is the basket I have plaited
for you, from strips torn out of the oldest monographs,
with the ocotillo's passion. Beneath me, buried in rubble,

a silver is waiting to be born into such commerce as belief
may lend. You may name it for my body when you
meet it by day at the judgment seat, by night on the narrow
road that sheathes my brother-song, green with pine
boughs I have stolen from death and death's trine passage.

On Setting Myself on Fire

"a myth has been terrifyingly corrected" —Yang Lian

○

The flesh is spoken to.
Duty calls the singe of concentration
unprintable names. The space between the body
& the body
blooms into not-being, not-
seeing how much surface breath can
bear. We want change, we say. This is change.

○

You raise your hand to the flames
because you desire
to hold them, to embrace them
like glass bells. They have come between you
& some idea of you, each rung
in turn by air's rapid plangency. O diapason.
You raise your hands as if you had
an answer to some question, or, cupped,
as if to receive some holy token.

○

Light writes on your hands, in terrible
script on the backs of your
beautiful hands, *Noli me tangere.* Forget myth,
the alphabet. Light's glyph imprints
directly. There is no "frame."
The cells are dying, men & women are dying
like cells
from the backs of your hands.

꽃

No one intervenes. No one wants to get
"too close"
& besides, it's fun to watch,
isn't it? To aestheticize. The eye is a distance
light intends to narrow.
You raise your hands to your eyes,
light's script a pucker, a retinal blur.
This all happens very quickly, understand.
This is not about reading.

꽃

Of course there is danger.
A part of yourself extends from the body
into air, which is suddenly a form
of light, unchained
from strict diurnal practice. Little suns,
come out from the forest
& play with us. We are so small & so
magnificently incomplete in our affections.

꽃

Flanked by fire the body feasts
on its own image, that lingua
franca of the ineffable. The table is set
in silver & porcelain. Everyone is happy, no
burden of tress or skeleton, only
the rich flesh
suffused with its intentions.
Bring on the pudding. Bring on the grail.

*Ghosts released from their wax
cylinders,* you think, stupidly beating
something like time
though it is not time. Everybody wants to see
what happens next. I'm a stranger here
myself, the body wants to say, &
Pass the ketchup. Some men
dive into the body
& never come back, not even for air.

Little suns, bring out your curious dead
so that we may strip them
of their studio recordings. So that we may
dress them in our pretty rags. Lining up
perception with perception, matter stumbles
into matter, the beveled edge
gives way to something sharp. It "catches,"
we say: song, body, reticule, flame.

It catches, & we turn: into, or against,
the air breathing something into us, not wings.
It makes such a beautiful photograph,
choice, &
we are so hungry, our hands & our clothing
are so lonely for what light
has to demonstrate. It all happens very
quickly, unaccompanied by music. Children,
cast your nets on the other side.

White Peaches

In darkness I move around my house
as a blind man might, touching
the walls, the furniture, small objects,
my own body. But this is not
blindness, this is darkness. A sheath
protects us from what is merciful.
On the kitchen counter, white peaches
plush in their basket of moonlight.
I must have bought them
but I can't remember where or when.
Little moons, come sing to me:
even gently, while winter surrounds
the blood's church, its brutal
angel. Let time be a music, a larger love
within snow's high architecture,
the saline cloth of prayerlight's city
voice. Fawns left almost beautiful
in blood-time mean something:
smallest dream, father-touch; meat-
touch, a glass sound. Faith
scars this god-field, friend, outside
memory (and other perfect waters).
Every being shares its gravity with us,
its cold ticking, the dense gift
sewn into day's garment of lidless eyes.
Once you heard a green music.
Did you reach out, then, salt-father?
Did you warm these globes
with your bare hand? As I
warm them now, severed against
all their radiant half-lives.
The pale flesh ripening, a velvet myth

in the register of ash, the treble
clef of ash. I am allowed to taste
each liquid rest exactly once.
Be matchgirl to my vagile orchard,
blind winter's compact gland
adrift in frost. How I succor love:
unribbed, as a third hand or balance—
the stone concealed in flesh,
its dim refulgence, a possession
I open my veins to, in regal splendor.

In Memory of Domestic Life

What is *heimlich* about stained glass is the way iron veins it, flame into orphanage. The logic of the ant is similar, interpenetration of matter with matter, what we call *earth*.

The body imagines a scale that is shaped like the body. It weighs itself, and then it weighs the Hebrew alphabet. Then it weighs itself again.

That *earth* can mean both *soil* and *planet* points up a difficulty with prepositions. We say *on* Earth and we say *in* the earth, even as the satellites watch.

In the house of the great poet needlepoint samplers were allowed to remain on the walls as memorials of an earlier time, an earlier metaphysic of solace-in-waking.

The igneous fusion of silicon with soda, potash, lime, or other chemicals we call *glass* exists without reference to or prejudice against the development of subsequent technologies, including both space flight and prepositions.

To the Greeks and Romans, prepositions existed primarily as stance, a point of view, a grammatical case: dative, ablative. Source, agent, cause, instrument.

The term for the systematic substitution of one vowel sound for another in different cases or derivatives of a verb is *ablaut*, coined by Jakob Grimm, of fairytale fame. Ring, rang, rung. It is also known as apophony, sound moving away.

Deep in their winter burrows, the ants dream of the satellites, though in their language of smell and touch they have no particular word for them. Satellites are just another form of *very-large-and-far-away*, of *not-enemy, not-food*.

In the house where the great poet lived the ghosts of the Greeks and Romans wander, picking up charred fragments of furniture here, fingering a hole in the plaster there. They remember the orifices of the body, the complicated alchemy of recognition and exchange.

The logic of concealment is the logic of inhument and resurrection. Alligators in the sewers, Al Capone's vault, believers gathering in the catacombs of Rome.

At some point stained glass became associated almost exclusively with the great edifices of the Christian church, a way of transforming light into story.

Once upon a time, wrote the Grimms, redacting the story of breath, which is different from the story of light. Source, agent, cause, instrument. Spring, sprang, sprung.

According to the news report, the buck crashed through the picture window and then, terrified, leapt crazily through all the rooms of the house, leaving an indecipherable scrawl of blood on the floors and walls.

In the house where the famous poet lived was a view of a green hill, and behind that hill, a mountain. There were shutters to keep the heat in, and the view out.

Deep inside the orphanage of the mind a church begins to wake, thread of ash, swatch of clockwork, a boat in the shape of a peony. *Listen,* it whispers. *There was a fertile valley, and in it two children, twins. And a wolf came unto them, and said . . .*

The body in its dreaming: *not-wave, not-particle,* neither math nor mineral, a vertical emphysema of the eye. It has forgotten something, about birds, maybe.

Movement toward or away from, time's Dopplered motion. The body shifts in the pure hospital of its private faith, its vault of respectable desecration. The prepositions cluster around the shallow pan of blood the glass slide holds.

In the stories, the orphanage is always burning. The ghosts run in and out, over and over again. They can't decide where they are supposed to be. The tongues of flame lick at them like manacles, oxygen pressing light from matter.

The body tries weighing a planet, on the one hand, and a story, on the other.

We say "the light of the eye," but we don't really mean it. We mean what greets us, strops us, buries us. We mean the shapes saints make in air.

On the Seventh Anniversary
of the U.S. Invasion of Afghanistan

Your body is a white palette
covering a sacrifice of gills, some moon's clement
misanthropy: I do not mean
it does not love us, only
                                that inside the ash-gold
camber physics makes, your breath exerts a gravity
trapped in winter's porcelain teeth
through which hunger like some history

keeps peering. The dogs run round & round
the salt well of your hair
barking—I almost wrote "banking"—

in the language of fur coats,
                                something already dead &
ornamental, a bamboo grove in January
offering its own guided tour

of the war, its broad cranium,
its massive hips. Sometimes I think
we are all figures in a portrait
                                            war is painting,
other times the canvas on which war paints.
If I say devotion is a candle
in the shape of a bell, you are already
six thousand miles away from the neighboring

        place setting, a French forest
through which soldiers sight
                                            my sister
bent low over thrust's smoking flare.
I like to imagine it—in this penultimate moment—

as a breathing thing, that turns in current,
          with eyes that magnify;
that feels pain after all, scientists now maintain.
What we call darkness, it calls desert.
Before language there was an *idea*
of language: to record
          the empathy, the mirage, the attractions

of both chance and surgery,
of *body* to *bomb*. The chapped hand of the one
who stoops now to trouble this water.

Chipping Campden

The light, being gold, does not end. The stone, being gold, does not end.

A gradual folding and unfolding, as a sheet of woven paper

that conceals some message of import—drawn out, read, and replaced

except that here one lives and breathes that testament, wrung like oil

from the evening's silk handkerchief. The flock gathers for its parliament

on the granite steps of the abandoned gatehouse, which in its turn

nods to the remaining pear and apple trees of the orchard.

It is too soon to pluck their fruit. I stand in the grass and judge

that it is too soon, even as I stretch my grasp towards the lowest branch.

My evening shadow falls on the ewes and lambs in the lower pasture,

gathered by the wall in rote expectation. To receive a message

is to participate in time, in the bright bonfire that is time's amanuensis.

Salt crusts beneath my collar as the breeze freshens.

I no longer have a working definition of the word "unnecessary,"

even as the will draws it from the mind, as with tongs. The fraternal lid

is semi-spherical, a dormitory for the coldest Abels

which I have left behind on another continent, without the anchor's

itinerant blue sheen. The light, being pastoral, sites the wick

in the snug flesh: of the man, of the beast, of the pear. I speak horizon

as a third language, hair fallen from the cheek of a reaped corpse.

Its grammar is sudden and brief. The ash tree gnaws it.

From the back entrance one may absorb the most stately absences,

the cleansing liniment, the fermata's half-root lingering

like an arum in damp ground. *Request news of love stop. Request quick, deft brasses to worry death's black beads in chancel stop.* Loom

as both toll and animal, to which the body is applied

as some fragrant butchery. We were warned off the site of life

as we are warned off the site of death. There is no time left,

I wrote, to frighten the children—you can look across,

into that empty laughter, towards which mercy aligns. In my dream

I did not contain enough blood to suit the needs of the people,

and so they cut my hair. They kept cutting it. The eye

of the sparrow, uncomprehending and volt-rinsed. It knows its own fear

which it carries aloft among the green rudders of the plain.

A meadow's golden spray, the civil depth of it, i.e. the separable soul

takes all too little space within the larger pattern. How it runs

now from the clatter in the lengthening dusk. This is the sermon

abundance kept preaching to us, while we were in the capital.

This is landscape's "likely prop of attention" from the curtailed charrette.

My arm is still raised, an image through which the pattern

flows. I want to craft from it a definition for "dwell." Dearest master,

I touch your green horn. You don't shed it and I don't

either, in any season. This we have in common: we are monsters.

We drink from the same pitted bowl. The wound, being gold,

does not end. The light, being gold, being wound in turn around faith's

glistening spindle, spends itself as a break in the cartilaginous vane.

Where there is intent there is security, that bludgeoning alloy.

Let us reenact the debt incorrectly, this time for charity's strabismic sake.

The burden of the valley of vision, which is to say, of shelter.

I lower my arm as if the object of my gaze had slipped from my sight.

Untitled (Drone Poem)

The general grief possesses us,
a desert music.

And the spirit of the frontier?

Pause and remember
the day we struck the movie set,
winter's wet planks.

You can buy
your own Rothko, penance signs.

Capitalism stumbles,
a bit,
in democracy's black chapel.

It sounds better as a duet.

We have created a city
for our best gods.
We have fed it our blue stories.

In the desert,
a honey clings
to isolation's woody branch.

Make your secret
classical, so that the bees
will bear it
out of Plato's cave.

How we select our leaders
persuades
faith's broad arroyo
in which a small church stands.

Its door is locked.

Bodies depart
from what is actual, the
molecular tithe.

This is how democracy happens,

on the bridge
overlooking
the former missile site.

It's a private movie,
playing in the old bank vault

over which
a prisoner of war
has painted a Western landscape.

The myth
is a symbolic anecdote,
Rothko wrote

from inside the war's
broad phylacteries, its distal
tracking shot:

—Christ's many secret deaths.

And do you feel
secure, penance asks
(in its thuggish blackletter).

Let me be gift to the gift-
makers,

a praying surface.

My hand among the lilacs,
my hand within the living Art.

Anniversary

(1)

The voyage to the anniversary was carpeted with the shed leaves of the peanut tree.

We walked to the anniversary on the legs of the tortoise and the giraffe. We sailed to the anniversary on barques made of India rubber.

The locomotive by which we reached the anniversary ran on a high rail of burnished acetaminophen.

All the bicycle paths led past the anniversary and on into a salubrious regret. Nevertheless we allowed the cyclists to pass our rickshaws, doffing our saffron tams in their various directions.

Flights into and out of the anniversary were much too expensive. The funicular railway and luge runs were options, when the weather was cold enough.

Some of us brought husbands, wives, lovers along. Some of us brought children, some brought dogs. One brought a pet parakeet in a jade cage.

The jungles that lay between us and the anniversary were said to be impenetrable. The deserts that lay between us and the anniversary were reported to be without oases, and inhabited by deadly scorpions and serpents.

The plains that lay between us and the anniversary were dotted with rosebushes whose thorns were said to be haunted. The swamps were whispered to have been drained and replaced by something even more dreadful, nobody knew quite what.

The intercepting mountains were very tall. Our horses stumbled on the rocky paths; the howdahs tipped crazily. Our chartered buses labored in the hairpin curves.

And always, beneath our feet, the shed leaves of the peanut tree.

(2)

For there to exist an anniversary two preconditions must be met: an aspect of reference, and a means of interval. The topography and disposition of any anniversary depends upon these necessary qualia.

In most cases the aspect of reference constitutes an Event, the means of interval a calendar.

Often, along the way to an anniversary, a new aspect of reference—a new Event— is added to memory, that is, adumbrated within the calendar.

This simply creates another anniversary.

Only rarely does a new means of interval interrupt a journey to an anniversary. It is more likely that a new means of transportation will present itself.

As we journeyed toward the anniversary we discussed these things.

The flickering of firelight against the liana at evening. The sirocco. The warm breath of the huskies in the snow.

(3)

During the day, from the backs of the camels and in subway cars and in the tumbrels pulled by oxen, we studied the protocols of the anniversary.

There was, traditionally, a sacrifice, of specie or livelihood. Likewise the superimposition of event upon Event, commemorative.

There would doubtless be certain local variations, oblique embroideries of culture, opportunities for error.

Distracted as we were by the frantic signaling of the castaways we must have missed some important points.

We understood that pilgrimages to the anniversary were often botched in the last possible moment. We understood that this was serious business.

And yet, looking up into the tangled nests of hummingbirds in the heart of some metropolitan constituency we felt our hearts lighten more than once.

For we perceived that the protocol of the anniversary unfolds inexorably along the journey, just as the journey itself is an essential aspect of that protocol.

We sang songs as we rowed, maintained moments of silence in the elevators.

(4)

There will be some who maintain that the anniversary is arbitrary, even mythical—that the literature of the anniversary is an elaborate hoax:

Either the precipitating Event never happened, or it did but its actual date and significance can no longer be fixed;

or else the means of interval, the calendar, is unreliable, owing to the sectarian tendencies of our major religious traditions or perhaps the almost imperceptible errancy of our planet as it slaloms through what we think of as space.

There will be, in the capitals, lecture series to denounce both the idea of the anniversary and the prospect of any journey.

There will be, in the rural districts, anathema pronounced by local shamans on those who either do or do not observe the protocols, the washings, the tithes of mint and cumin, the tying of threads.

It is so easy to lose track of such things.

Over the centuries many guidebooks have been written, even published, providing advice, commentary, maps. When the weather was good, we read these books with interest. When the weather was bad, we fed their pages to our fires.

(5)

Once, while fording a treacherous mountain cataract, it occurred to me that we might have missed the anniversary entirely and moved on, like the cyclists, into regret.

I mentioned this to my remaining companion, who merely laughed.

We had been warned that although the water looked bracing and clear, it contained leeches, and the current was swift and deadly. We had even been taught, by the locals, a charm to murmur, in a singsongy sort of voice, as a prophylactic against either the leeches or the current, or perhaps both.

It is with great grief and—yes—regret that I confess to you I no longer recall the words or the melody to that charm.

You will suggest I contact my erstwhile companion, whose memory might exceed mine. Or that perhaps together we will be able to piece together what we each, individually, have lost.

When we parted, it was a cloudy day. A warm wind from the south stirred the volcanic ash of the plain, flecking his parka and my beard.

Flocks of pelicans wheeled overhead, dark stars in a milky sky.

(6)

There is of course more to say on the subject of sacrifice, also the disposition and relative plenitude of food and lodging along the most-traveled routes;

about the help we received, and the many obstacles that were laid in our paths;

about the shadows cast by those who made the journey, and the prismatic effect of certain cloud formations; about both light and its interruption.

At night, as we slept, we often cried out, dreaming.

And always, underfoot,

      beneath the tires and the snowshoes,
      used as bookmarks,
      encrusted in the fossilized shale,
      clinging to the stiff coats of llamas or the welcome mats of teahouses,
      buried with corpses for good luck,
      encased in pastry,   pounded into papyrus,
      distilled into ink or unguent,
      folded gently into aromatic stews or used as currency
      or else floating on the surface of those waters—

gift-sprung cynosure, unburdening cathexis, prayer to Mnemosyne half-mumbled
at the immense amethyst altar of waking, as of sleep—

the fact of that laughter. And the shed leaves of the peanut tree.

Convocation (Psaltery)

The skin is precogniscient; man is not.
Banking sharply hundreds of feet
over the trainyards of Chicago, east of us
the blue doffs like the ocean it's
technically not & I burnish what's left
of my memories of you. They're a small
town, & getting smaller with the passage
of years, like Dunwich undercut
& calving off into its saline estuary,
taking lewd skeletons with it. We can go
down into the North Sea's frigid dark
with the right equipment & photograph
the toppled strata, seismic & wave-
frowzed. Sometimes touch is better
than illumination, as in that black water.
Yesterday I heard someone say
one mark of culture is whether people
think trains are worth watching,
as a form of entertainment. Your father
used to take you down to the local
siding on June evenings lacquered
with cicada. *If I say a ghost or a deer,*
both are true, Mei-Mei Berssenbrugge
writes. When Christ arrived on the shores
of Lake Michigan, the people
knew Him, my neighbor insists. Now
I am glazing you from sand & fire & some
chemical that may resemble lymph,
or blood. How the light passes *through*
the body, an occult wave function.
Far below we are dismantling the smallest
economies. It is not as painful

as it should be. There you are, real again
in the leaded windows of a church.
Love butchers me at these altitudes
& I hear your quiet voice asking *Do you
want the liver, or the lungs, or the heart.*

Neither Winter nor a Golden Dust

Now in the night I lie crippled again and know
even less about mercy. Like flesh stopped
against the soul's brief song we enter the house
of the forest-warden, a closed bread, hostel
for such as come by train or with a pilgrim-
's staff and satchel. I am not a pilgrim and yet

I, too, belong here, among the laurel and the ash.
Adrift within my infirmities I succor
what small sparks hew me-wards, micro-lives
to which my body is the knowing macroverse.
What a pity it is, I think, they do not
sing, or not in any human register. I brush them

as a god must, lying prone in perfect pain;
belief sounds this way from any great distance.
As a watch in the night I am lacking:
this bed, the filtering star-bracts, my own blood
are all more perfectly in tune with oxygen
than any specie I could will against debt's war.

The master of the house is elsewhere, no sound
reaches me through the plastered laths;
he has taken his wife and children with him—
thus does hope circulate between worlds,
leaving its shiny tracks on my dawn-side pelt.
From his ragged shelf of books I choose

the one I guess most wedded to my service,
bound in char and in the tongues of hares
that undermine this tenement—but the pages

are, it seems, uncut; the pads of my fingers
leave damp whorls on the night's black lens.
A thin layer of grit, or pollen, coats everything

memory has genuflected to, but my mantle
is somehow the same actinic white I struck
from the heart's brined cell. I've cast it aside,
for the night's sake, on a sturdy chair
which means I write these lines in naked faith.
Rod and cone daven in the electric light

until, deprived of those twin chantries, the mind
collapses like a desert tent. I will lie like this
in the chamber of my ligaments until bells
heal my purchase with their frailing apothegms.
Let my frame be a honey-stanchion then,
a sill, a dry milk. Some fragrant ballast crashing.

Fishguard Harbour

There is a moment prayer occurs
to the conscious mind, or rather
the absence of prayer in the moment of need
hitherto. Experience names the vacuum
it has been seized by,
only the mouth—
the physical fact of the mouth,
sensuous, capable of beauty or deceit—
can't form the words
the ventral thalamus is telegraphing.

And all the poets were very serious,
the poets of Ireland, the poets of Wales
in the face of this
new century,
seethed in mother's milk. It is all very ironic
or else very far away, those childhoods
of synagogues & ash,
harsh words,
flesh peeled from the left index finger
by a tin-snip's errant jag.

Remorse is not the same as prayer.
Regret, the soul's oblation
to emptiness: soliloquy
to the unknown god, that Mars Hill
catch-all. We're sorry, we say
to no one in particular,
the dark lorries, the gorse-studded cliffs.
Sorry, the dumb bones of the saints
whisper back
from their bruised ossuaries,

a kind of light—corposant, St. Elmo's fire—
the names of the dead
(if not the dead themselves)
keep right on seeking. It is not enough
to be indifferent to the body,
its trine majority, its fungible relation.
A cold mist fronted in
from the harbor, every molecule
bristling, alive—so the Greeks maintained—
with motes from a Perceiver's eye.

Eight Short Films about Architecture

(1)

In the middle of the night certain noises resolve themselves into raccoons, mice, ghosts, or else the proverbial settling of the house, the implication of architecture.

Architecture may be defined as the spatial arrangements of occupancy, that is, the myriad if particular ways of remaining where one already is.

A diurnal architecture resolves itself into windows, feints at the attractive illusion that architecture itself is not real. That architecture in the act of revealing itself reveals, in fact, something else, its own absence.

Certain vectors tangent to architecture may include both tenure and transportation. Each of these is responsible for directing its own sublimation into form.

A nocturnal architecture, on the other hand, may involve the improvisational performance of any number of beings and vectors whose admission to the premises cannot be vouched for. Bruce Nauman produced intricate films of such performances.

Film, of course, being itself an architecture, aesthetically pleasing merger of day and night.

To the extent the performativity of film occurs within time we may say that a film's architecture is tangent to that of the body. To the extent the performativity of film depends upon the movement of structures, bodies, and currencies along and within a commercially predictable set of causeways and labyrinths we may say that a film's architecture is tangent to that of motion.

Outside my house, in the dark, the old carriage shed, later a garage, empty now, glitters like a film that has not been shown in many years. The celluloid has begun to decay.

To turn the camera outward from the fact of architecture, rather than inward, is to admit the possibility of a larger architecture. This notional architecture would include, for instance, automobiles and satellites and fast food vendors, those inimitable exteriors.

It is possible that all architectures, everywhere, are tangent to one another. One leaves a building only to enter its neighbor. A continual entering and exiting.

(2)

In some films, a raccoon gets into an argument with a ghost at night. In others, a ghost becomes entangled with the settling of a structure into its foundations.

The raccoon, as scavenger, is always an extra.

The nature of night is to provide a backdrop against which the diurnal apprehension of light can be made perceptible, tangible, real. This is less a matter of warding off ghosts than of providing some confirmation of each person's belief in the other's existence.

In some films, ghosts are real people. In some films, real people are ghosts.

The purpose of night lighting is to illuminate the bodies of others, that is, to make them real by positioning them within a film. Most nights come equipped with soundtracks: crickets, sirens, pop music. Sometimes just the whir of the camera.

It could be argued that sound itself occupies during the night the same position a physical body occupies during the day, that is, as a nearly tactile ghost of itself. Were this true, however, the extras would have no speaking parts.

A man or a woman walking alone down an otherwise empty street during the day constitutes one kind of film. A man or a woman walking alone down an otherwise empty street during the night constitutes another.

One of the conventions of the American horror film is the reassuring agency of precognition assigned to the viewer but denied the actors in their roles. *Here it comes,* or *Don't go down there!* The heroine opens the door to the dark basement just as a creaking sound is heard. It could be the house, the wind, a mouse.

Don't go down there! Of course she goes down there. It's almost always that sort of film.

(3)

Like a firebell in the night. The film the U.S. Civil War made was a long one. Only the stills survive, shot by Matthew Brady, who infamously posed the corpses.

There is one school of film theory which teaches that corpses are themselves films, inanimate films (as opposed to films of the inanimate), i.e. each corpse presupposes a drama that will remain forever locked into the fact of a body until that body decays. The decomposition, of course, constitutes an entirely separate, and competing, film.

Another school of film theory holds that the corpse—that is the human body, deprived of sentience, reduced to meat—becomes its own extra, or even a prop. It ceases to be its own film and becomes a mere token in another film.

There are, of course, those who argue that every corpse is simply a film within a film, in the same way that every stone contains an infinite number of smaller stones locked impenetrably inside.

Transportation into and out of such films may be arranged in advance, with or without the knowledge or consent of the director. Admission is free.

(4)

The American road movie is one perennial sign of our national obsession with architecture. The car chase, which is in fact the American road movie speeded up and interpellated within the body of another narrative for adrenaline's sake, performs this same function.

As an element of architecture the American automobile is unsurpassed. There may, in the end, be only so many ways of living inside the film of one's own journey.

Closely related to the American road movie is the American buddy movie. Many road movies are buddy movies, and vice versa. The reason for this is parallax: two seemingly independent points of view may provide more satisfactory corroboration of the architecture they purport to inhabit.

The weakest moment in either an American road movie or an American buddy movie always comes when the duo is separated, or becomes separated from the relevant, projecting architecture. For instance, the bank-robbing scene in *Thelma & Louise.*

It is instructive to note that in fact the bank-robbing scene in *Thelma & Louise* plays twice, first off-camera from the point of view of a non-witnessing non-participant, then as a flashback from the point of view of a security camera. The actual robbing of the bank is thus an invisible film within a film, that is, a corpse.

Both scenes are preceded by a scene in which a third party explains the finer points of bank robbing to the eventual robber, but this scene is never actually shown in the film.

(5)

In Bruce Nauman's cinematic explorations of architecture the camera, fitted out with infrared technology, is allowed to run in the artist's studio overnight. The result is a study in duration through which various insects, mice, cats, etc. travel.

Duration being yet another architecture, yet another film extending, accordion-like.

It could be argued that the three-dimensional space of the studio (four, if you count duration) is the central component—protagonist, if you will—of Nauman's project, in which the assorted non-human visitors count as extras. Or, it could be maintained that Nauman himself is obviously the project's subject, even though he remains physically absent from most of the films.

The problem with remaining absent within one's own film is essentially that of *habeas corpus,* most often translated "who has the body?" (but which actually means "you shall have the body").

Time is always a problem in film, as in architecture. We want to believe that architecture is timeless because we prefer to see it as objective, discrete.

The problem with time in architecture is time's intent to reduce architecture to a corpse, that is, to a film in which time itself plays no role.

Thus, architecture on some level is always a film in which the director, Time, is standing just beyond the capture of the lens.

Which is not to neglect the possibility that within the purview of architecture the camera itself may come to occupy a subjective position relative to that of the film, become a corpse itself. Typically we refer to such instances as nostalgias, another architecture altogether.

(6)

When I was a child I lived in a large house with an attic fan whose choppy rhythm regulated my nights and whose poor wiring threatened more or less continually to burn the house down.

(It is possible, at this point in this film, to cue the Talking Heads video "Burning Down the House," in which a fire is projected, via film, onto the lateral exterior of a house, and which I first saw, on television, in the house with the erratic attic fan.)

When I was a child I would occasionally mistake the choppy rhythm of the fan for a prowler. This added interest to an otherwise desultory narrative arc.

Once, alone in the house at dusk, I was sufficiently spooked by the narrative possibilities of cinema that instead of investigating the basement or the attic I fled, out into an open area where two streets crossed. There I constructed an elaborate hydraulic model of our house from rain-washed silt that had collected in the intersection. When my parents returned to the neighborhood, long after the sun had set and the streetlights had come on, this is where they found me.

A street, of course, is the architecture in which motion finds purest residence. A lane, a highway, an avenue, a boulevard. Each its own genre, its own gesture towards flight.

On another occasion, alone in the house after dusk, I in fact mistook footsteps in the front hall for the choppy rhythm of the attic fan: until I saw the body-shaped shadow falling across the entrance hall from the well-lit door of the bathroom. The shadow appeared to be holding something—a subsidiary shadow—in its hands.

Some flights, like some bodies, move towards the camera; some flights move away. At such moments we remark that it is "bright as day" or "dark as night." These clichés assist in the construction of a comforting architecture within language.

Between my body and the entrance to the hall was the kitchen, and on the kitchen counter was a set of knives my father kept razor-sharp. I drew the longest knife and approached the shadow.

(In the music video, the band members are successively, and with apparent violence, replaced by extras, who may be meant to symbolize alter egos, or may just be passing through.)

I approached the shadow in the hallway with confidence, with a knife in my hand. The attic fan clanked and whirred. The door to the basement remained closed.

(7)

According to some theorists weather may be classified as an architecture. This is incorrect; weather is a medium through which architecture, like film, incurs.

In part the confusion stems from the imbrication of the diurnal-nocturnal cycle with meteorological conditions. Both affect the quantity and the quality of light, and therefore the sorts of architecture that may be defended or destroyed.

In light snow, for instance, films portraying the bodies of small children may be produced, though not shown. In heavy snow, films portraying explosions may be shown, but not filmed.

It is more appropriate to suggest that weather, in the context of cinema *qua* architecture or architecture *qua* film, is another corpse, another extra. Another honkeytonk bruiser or expendable teen.

Weather may become the agency through which even the most elaborate architecture is reduced to rubble, that is, absence. A leak in the roof, a tornado, a flood.

When weather opens the door to the dark basement, we root for the basement. When weather takes control of the camera, we draw our knives from their belted sheaths.

Most urban legends resolve themselves around questions of lighting and set. The lovelorn suicidal Munchkin in *The Wizard of Oz* is just a shadow, or a reflection, or possibly an exotic bird. The spectral boy in *Three Men and a Baby* is a cardboard cutout.

Both scenes were shot in broad daylight, hence the confusion and the resolution.

Night, on the other hand, poses as another story, another film. *Don't go down there!* we shout to the lone teen in the dark house, on a dark road, about to make a bad decision. If only there were independent points of view to corroborate the action.

We think, *safety in numbers,* but it never works out this way. We think, *If I were there, I'd know what to do,* but it never works out this way, either.

Down she goes.

(8)

Celluloid, like buildings, burns. The speed of the burning depends upon the material, also upon the rate at which the combustion is filmed.

In childhood it always struck me as useful to distinguish between "fear of the dark" and "fear of what's *in* the dark." Architecture, like film, locates such fears.

The fact of a ghost is meaningless—without valence of fear—outside the structures afforded by architecture. Ghosts haunt: houses, cemeteries, forests. They are autochthonous: they keep within the architecture they themselves define.

To decant a ghost is to denature the ghost.

Fire is thus one of the few elements of modern cinema that cannot on some level be reduced to the office of corpse. Fire in movies, as in life, must, and minimally, occupy the role of ghost. (Thus, the horror film trope of using fire to deter zombies.)

To be haunted by fire is to find oneself in the grip of a film, of which architecture is merely agent, an outward manifestation. Even the buddies in buddy movies must spend their nights somewhere: in their cars, in tents, in cheap roadside motels.

Fear of architecture: no word in the dictionary. Fear of film: *cinemaphobia?*

In the films in which buildings burn there is almost always, and also, a fear of falling, which is to say, of the basement's rising from its subterranean effacement, of night's obtrusion into day. Plane crashes, terrorist attacks. *Crash and burn,* the saying goes.

In film the explosion of all architectures simply becomes another architecture.

Outside my house, in the dark, ice ticks against the storm windows, the old carriage shed, the stained slate of my roof, the bricks of the street, the chassis of my Toyota. Parked and ready. In the basement, the furnace lights, purrs, cuts out, lights, purrs, cuts out again.

That noise: raccoons in the garbage. Or a siren. Or a ghost. Or the house settling. Or—nothing. It could be nothing. The camera is running. The sleeper is stone.

Candleweb, Thaw

In prelude the night moves
its stiff sentience away
from the windowsill you call
Marry me, a story the sky
diffracts as if it were
a telegram, unbuttered toast.
We are not sentinels
here, in this unfolding larch
of wax crowns riven
with cropmarks pissed
listlessly by winter
wolves. A movie concludes
with a call from the stage-
struck set of Pentecost
unplowed & lightly elemental,
O my unbuttoned birds
the monster rains moan &
how we bandage them,
little jack pine traps prinking
for the ambient. You
are never empty & I thank
every more recent idea
for the dross & moon-
glitter that illuminates this
percussive efference,
Rose of Sharon blossoms
fitted into their hollow
breviaries, a new leather
is what it says in the guide-
book, this & other
haptic angles developed
in lieu of how lucky

we are to hold the lamp-
child so that in the streetlight's
broth-strobed paraflection
its arms appear to be
both moving & indifferently
on fire, unbroken, alive.

Map

(after Jasper Johns)

The mouth opens.
Do something to it. Do
something else to it.
Music music. No I had
not seen the monkeys.
We are all cages
of meat. Anything
isn't more interesting.
A sluice. A palace.
Starshine of Canton.
What isn't. There
by the text-fountain.
We try to remove
the spar from the ship.
Beware the body.
Beware the mind's
slow animal, its polar
hum. *O.* Unthinking
watchman. Try
harder. The monkeys
screaming. Into
the perfect s(w)erve.
We must remember.
To infect, via touch.
It is not so small.
It is not so iridescent.
You had a dream I say,
a pearling growth.
The state is an object.
Blot the cage. Only
tarry. For a little
while. For a signature.
Hello hello hello.

Soldiers in the news.
The skin stretched,
almost invisibly.
Over the breast. Over
the marked breast.
As soap or newspaper
traps. The lying I.
In the present tense.
No secret intelligence.
The plaster calf
adrift from its upland,
fall or worship.
Sleep sleep cheeps
the monkey's sex.
Their smell a parallax.
A rebus. A red
diagnostic. Piecemeal
into the blind fire.
You are not a spy.
Inside the cage a seam
extends, a pure heat.
Varicose. Welded.
Place your wax inside
the thigh's blue
hour. Ennumeraled.
Our underlying
structure, pierced.
Depends. Suspends.
The dancers move
within the plane. O
dreamless willow.
The budding clock
stenciled in dusk.
You can't "watch" it.
You are not a fire.
You are not a laundry,

a quince, a spline.
Kepler dismounts,
ripe from insect time.
Hello hello hello.
Signs the scented hand.
Signs the fountain's
scapula. Avid. Imma-
culate. Dry & sewn.

Poem in Which I Pretend You Are Still Alive (I)

Far below, the snow is learning.
What does the snow learn?

We fly through lightning.
Lightning is the total poem
as poetry (Adonis) is the wind's rose,
the blood borne
only on an invisible wind.

What does the snow learn?
The shape of the flesh,
the shape of the heat of the flesh
and its offal.
The sun is a distant body,
six-fingered.
They stare across at one another.

The snow's heart
is the sun's myth, and vice versa.

Your body: lacking
in amenity, or lacking in vital
spark—the doubling
life of you
prayer-bled, out
as if an exhalation of stones.

Six-fingered, some curious god
feels the lemons in
the marketplace, pale little earths.

We make ourselves at home
in the burning city
of the body, its clepsydral tent
frailing a blue instrument.

That city is burning,
we say. —No, *that* city.

What I am saying is,
The wound through which the rose
enters the body
is very small. Almost anything
could cause it:
a bullet, a mirror, a spear
tipped in cardamom,
honey—

Far below, the snow is learning.
We fly through that terrible light.

Poem in Which I Pretend You Are Still Alive (II)

City on the ground
whose glyph I cannot read,
forgive me.
We cannot all be light.

I return to cardamom
because it is the soul's
next spice,
its jealous lover.

(My dairy-farming friend,
smelling it for the first time,
said
"It is not of this world.")

City on the ground,
love burns pure love away
until only love is left,
a terrible lotion
of light, & breath, & ash.

We die, a little, when we
see it
in the museums
and the marketplaces.

In one museum,
you may take love down
from the wall, and hold it,
for a little while.
Docents lift it
gently from your palms

which, of course,
are now covered in scars.

City on the ground,
I carve you
into the rough skin
of my thigh, into
the back of my left hand.

(The poets will think
it is some stylish tattoo.)

The scar leaves a beautiful
scent
when light touches it,

when the memory of light
severs
the ripe pear from its
low branch, the flat scape
of breath
from the body

as if it, too, were to blame.

The Prescriptivist

We were walking through Nevada,
through one of those towns in Nevada
that might as well be a ghost town
although people still live there.
Some of them are physicians. Some
are high school students, *Go Team.*
Some of them were trying to resurrect
the old gold mines. It made them filthy
and I was wanting to interview
a few for some project or other inside
a solid, early 20th-century building
that looked more like a courthouse
or abandoned school. It was the pithead.
Enormous gears revolved around us
while we spoke, calf-thick cables
of braided wire. It was a hard life,
they conceded. This much we agreed on.
Then I noticed the reddish welts
on my forearms: somehow I'd acquired
a parasite. I needed medical attention.
When something goes wrong
with the body there is this temptation
to take hold, *squeeze.* As if pressure
were what the body wanted, all along.
The mind a parasite in its chitin
bowl, its paperweight retablo. And so
I missed the accident, the crowd
gathered there, the broken windows.
It was all very still. I didn't "get it"—
There should be gouts of flame
I told my wife, stupidly. (I had a wife.)
We were at the hospital then.

I'd milked the body of its public
guest. It was disgusting, though also
it felt good. *What happened to the children*
is what you wanted to know:
my children, our children, the miners'
children. It was that kind of town,
Rose of Sharons darning the hedgerows,
songlines worn to dusty amphorae.
Ambient wounds, you called them.
How the whole mountain, hollowed out
for waste, would sound, if you struck
it. And you struck it. With an iron
rod. The way the players advanced
across the field, as if they were invisible
trees in a visible forest, or pure metals
crucified into an alloy, something
useful. That we could handle.
There was no music, nothing to call
aesthetic, that is, the beautiful—only
old snow at the higher elevations
layered with a dream of snow.
And the charred faces of the crowd
crowning like a king into the birth
assembly, a pale king in his infant flesh
expecting adoration, expecting
the human breast. Warm and smooth.
Or like a currency. Something raised
from great depths by the body's
will, its sheer (com)passion for what it
cannot have, cannot incorporate.
You lift it to your face, your white
chest. Even as the onlookers applaud.

Small Song (for Edith Stein)

Quick sprout the songbird. Beads of ash on ash gather in limbs, in the pleats of
the curtain thick limbs make. Quick sprout the songbird and its mate.

Quick sprout the nightbird. The stars have fallen and burn from the pavements,
sharp, glary, discarded chemist's tools. Quick sprout the nightbird by its Yule.

Quick sprout the daybird. Biology's thunder strikes spears from hunters' hands, the
wet spoon from the mother's. Quick sprout the daybird from its milky gutter.

Quick sprout the redbird. Its heart fills a scabbard with its needle of tongue. They
quarrel like lovers. Quick sprout the redbird and the redbird's young.

Quick sprout the shybird, hid in plexure's soft folds. Clever hands prick and pluck
with insects' skill. Quick sprout the shybird from the bone-bright till.

Quick sprout the waybird. Amid spoiled bedding lies a bicycle wheel, plastic head
of a doll. One sandal. Quick sprout the waybird and the waybird's call.

Quick sprout the Maybird, vast mother of weddings. Euclid fills the pond, drains
it, fills it again. Quick sprout the Maybird in its coat of flayed skin.

Quick sprout the smallbird. From waxy cells bees tender their last dances. The
retinas steal what language can't keep. Quick sprout the smallbird and its
sibilant meat.

Quick sprout the earthbird. Rubble treasures up its midden's currency: white
chocolate left for lunatics, or Jews. Quick sprout the earthbird in mendicant fury.

Quick sprout the drybird. Where children walked now soldiers swim like gnats; a
duchess pries the jewels from her husband's teeth. Quick sprout the drybird
and the thief.

Quick sprout the bluebird's box, and the bluebird's narrow vest. One man's purpose
is another's rough relation. Quick sprout the bluebird from St. Thomas's chest.

Quick sprout the gyrebird and its cousin, the hawk. Their hoods are a justice. They
breed in their sleep. Quick sprout the gyrebird under heaven's red speech.

Quick sprout the charbird. A bucket brigade bears bent scalpels, soiled cloths:
in and out of the surgery. All musics stop. Quick sprout the charbird from
its dark knot.

Cancer Poem

I was a child there. And milk taught me
how to draw with a war in my hand.
I felt God as a nerve
running through the copper sky.

The trees sang to it, especially the oaks
that guarded winter's altars.
Everyone was afraid of time's groin,
against which the town rubbed up

whenever the moon lost at snow.
My breath was a glass
inside of which a single blossom hung,
Friendship viewed me as prey,

a dead calm afflicting the hospitals
built on the site of an ancient
wheel. Who has the magic hand
that will illuminate

the stubborn light inside a snail's shell?
No one had died but those we loved,
those we'd sent away from us
that we might grasp the yellow falcon

by its jet, Sephardic talons.
Tubes were fitted into our worst art
through which the glory-salt
emanated. There was a brief period

during which all the wounded
bore the same name, a single letter

removed from my own . . . As a child
I played at the edge of a veil,

I counted the accidents
that did not happen beneath the bank's
percussive shadow. Now
night lures night's Philadelphias

to the tips of my chest,
where they burn. Thus I am stripped
of mercy's caul, I am laid open
to love's blue braid

and the town is my Lucifer
bearing its lame sine-vow before it.
What makes the animals animals
is that they don't fear losing

you. O Father, I would burst
into coal for You, I would darken—
Let honey's rude periphery
tune the land's guitar, its anti-psalm.

The Fear Was in the Northeast

The fear was in the northeast.
We watched it coming in low
like a jetliner. No, you said,
like a flock of starlings. No,
you said, like a single bird of prey
or like a dark balloon
or like some new form of weather.
No, you said, while the fear
continued to move toward us,
toward where we were.
Where we were was wet
and we could feel the onrushing
of the fear against our cheeks,
which were exposed, against
our bare necks. It made them burn,
the way roses burn. No,
you said. The way barns burn.
The way hydrants burn.
And there was just enough time
for this. And we had a name for it,
a name that made another place
for us, the way photographs do.
We tried to photograph the name.
The drops cold on our faces
like faces. No, you said.
This is the thing we called a face.
And it was not like anything.
And we were inside it.
And the fear passed over us
like an issue of blood, or like smoke.
And the light was different, after.
And we rubbed our tusks

against it. To see the sparks.
And we agreed on this,
that we should call it *the body,*
rather than, say, *the river.*
And we really wanted to see
it, too. But the face was setting.
And we had burned the photographs.
Lost them. Discarded them.
Defaced them, with acid or soot.
No, you said. Here they are.

Common Prayer

Prayer is a harrow. No iambs or incentives, no cherubim, no majuscule illumination. The hero stirs from his bed of the mind, blinks in drowsy sunlight. The risk of talking to God is that He may talk back, or else remain silent.

The forest is not a biddable place. Comes the harrow.

Beloved, whispers the paper birch, and then continues in its insensible tongue. We, rapt, grasping at its supple branches, choose to hear *Beloved, beloved, beloved.*

The logic of dryad, of hamadryad is speech into speechlessness.

Prayer says: beneath this birch a soldier once executed a prisoner with whom he had been charged, because he did not wish to be inconvenienced on his way to the capital. Or, from the branches of the tree from which the seed that proved this birch once fell hung the body of a man whose feet had been burned with fire, whose genitals savaged.

The forest is not a biddable place. Comes the harrow.

It is comforting to think of the forest as a thread, thread of wood, one among many, this weaving into immanence. Casting pardon, and not always to speak.

We make patterns in language as smiths strike nails: heat, draw, hammer. Language is like a house after a fire, its halo of iron and lead. Or: like a beautiful dress with the needles and pins left in. Or: like a beautiful dress made of lead, after a fire.

The reason the angels are deaf is so that words spoken in greatest ecstasy or despair might reach God alone. The reason the angels are blind is to discourage their thieving instincts.

In the forest, theft is accomplished without reference to the senses. Xylem, phloem, photosynthesis. Ligature, fold. Theft is structure.

In the oldest stories, prayer is the fire by which the hero consumes the heroine. It is the field after the forest has been felled, also the instrument for the preparation of that field. It is an implement of teeth and of the spaces between teeth. A mangle and a map.

What love permits, in the end, is not the dispersal of the echo, but the dispersal of the hero. See him disappear into the forest piece by piece, into his palaces of celluloid and wax.

Prayer says: if you hang a new door I will batter it down. If you batter down the door I hang I will seal you in.

Prayer says: I am the residue of love.

Theft is structure. The forest is not a biddable place. Whispers paper birch and nightingale, the mistral and the sparrow, frail anemone. Comes the harrow.

Passion for St. Wenog's Day

My hand passes over the braille of the frost and erases it, clay legend to the body's
map of betrayal, its private audience. Again and again the chosen leave by night
for distant safeties. Under no spirit of debt does the violet suspend its script
beneath the heart's thirsty meat-level. I have been left behind, in the precinct
of the lathe's ecstatic blindness. To dwell within the fixed bounds of the procession
is to stumble in tune with the breath's held note, gold coin in the paradise-rafter.
Thus does our heat move out from us. Everything exiled is visible from the air
in season of drought: funerary monuments, the amerced habitations. Make straight
the succor offered the grieving haunch of the locust's bole. God defines mercy
in terms of mercy, tautologically—in a dark room, a spirit drawing, a double exposure.
We miss our dead and their green crimes. Turn again in the river like the great
carp that needs no baptism, that bears our sin in its cancerous brow. I have eaten
the substance of beings that felt fear and pain. The print of my palm against winter's
bastard page—by way of deposition, a purebred vintage. My brother bears the scar
of harvesting in his tongue. I have never seen his signature. I have seen him
carve stiff muscle from the spine, have watched him scrape an orchard
from the bluff's glazed plait. He that hath two coats, let him impart to him
that hath none. The new year christens itself with the old year's X. I have directed
the mourners to their plastic seats. The slowest dance is the violet's embanked
chromosomes, from which I'm barred. Down on all fours now, on ground
my beard and breath brush and polish. As I warm the grass I also block the light.

Watching Sparrows Dust-Bathe in a Dry Gutter

Look into the cave left by the blind tongue. Beside me and behind me each tune
like a miniature sea, plumbed with salt. The prayers of the dead press against
the pallet of breath, that smoked glass beyond which the sun's deaf corona flares.
The perpetual green thought of winter flecks the vein, unreadable neumes
scratched in vellum. My students can't distinguish their bodies from the dawning
page. They toss and turn. I offered to burn my brother's map, so outdated
it marked each infirmity with an integer rather than a name. He was on his way
to his nephew's wedding. What's spelled in the lungs' Carolingian uncials
is no signature. I cut my own hair at midnight—mirror in one hand, scissors
in the other—rather than have another man's wife touch me. My ex-lover kneels
in the same room as her new lover. This is astonishing. I sleep with a long knife
at my bedside, by the glass of water. These words are shadows, a detached wing
left bloody at the turnout. In the cave you can see where the hunters set a fire.
You can't tell what language they spoke. You can't tell whether they suffered.
I break the toy across the flat of my thigh, let its sharp edges prick my flesh.
In the shadow play it's what they left behind, neither meat nor debt nor trophy.

The Grievers

Granted, chance plays a role: the right verb of motion, the map
in which the body is wrapped. A man grasps his god by its forelegs and throws it
      across his shoulders, its muscles
distended, meat-jewels in a bronze crown. What the gods use fire for in our lives
      is to reveal everything, minutely if briefly.
It is not enough to have a voice, a form, a nerve threading its way
through the migrant forest. First we are lost, and then the letters begin to arrive
      addressed in a meticulous hand.
Your shoulders, twin dark lamps, ache. The wood you have gathered thrums
      in common with what has been taken from you.
Each man binds his burden, some to the bodies of women, some
      to the bodies of beasts.
Snow flecks the evergreens. Your path leads directly through
where flame was, or soon will be. At least you're not alone here. The light
      traces legends on the strong ground, a sheaf,
a ship, an alphabet, a homonym. We were warned, of course. All these apparels
      the eye follows, to the belly and further, enough
flesh for everyone. I want but forget to ask for the architect's name.

The Doubled Organs

Lungs, kidneys, testes,
the eyes, fine-spun apparatus
of the middle & inner ear;
no chronology in the
body's bilateral symmetry.
Remember the tombstones
made of flame, the flesh-
pistons of the starlings
lifting from the field at dawn.
You cannot pass. You
cannot touch, with the hand,
certain edges of the body.
A ladder is a vertical
rigor, love's imperfect
tense. Strengthen the debt,
the myriad attractions.
Preposition *vs.* proposition,
when God is watching
vs. when God is "when."
As a door opens or closes
seemingly by itself
means a storm is coming.
What is found *vs.* what
is believed to have been lost.
When we walk on water
it means the water's ice.
Repent of the whole body
on the body's grounds:
a mansion, richly appointed.
Here is a golden lamb, &
here is the fingernail
of a saint. The soul walks
into the body the way

three men walk into a bar,
only it is no joke. *You*
cannot pass. The starlings'
flailing ore against the wind's
dumb recompense, a red
depth, like light or volume.
When we were children
we played in the cemetery.
We leapt over the stones.
Love lathes love's blue
accident, its Caesar-throne.
Be as gold, as vitrine. As one
impressed for mourning.

What David Taught & Where He Taught It

I no longer have the plan within me. —Any plan.
I am no longer able even to weep.
(Was that part of the plan? Surely it was.)
Where I tended a garden a verb has taken shape:
a poison masquerading as honey. I buy & I buy
calendars, all of them missing days—
days I can't remember or else remember much
too well. I had never thought the past
would come to me in the shape of a bell,
a bird, a bone: that is, brailled and charming.
No I have never driven the combine, the chopper,
the harvester. I see my ghost-fingers in the chaff,
pale & bloody, little Christs. A tray
of surgical instruments glitters at the far edge
of my dusky solfege. Is this a plan? No,
this is a machine, & the angel of machines
has come to trouble all that yet lies
within me. I feel its breath, a library cold & heavy
on my bearded cheek. How to believe
in something that is not already a part of oneself?
—The way the garment believes in the body
as long as it's being worn; the way I take
the poison into myself for the sake of its sweetness.
Plan, from the Latin *planus,* flat. A schematic
of where love has dwelt, the apposed weft's
blue inclusory. I protected nothing, I bloodied
my apron with love's tenses. My children
burn like matchsticks in a single night.
They sound their one note like trumpets wrapped
in gauze . . . Speak ark, speak ash. You
who do not know how to die, who read this,
you whose standing perturbs the unnaillable light.

Ascension Day

The visions that open up lie within visions
and they are thin: Christ
as field-of-hands; the burning orchard;
the abandoned (or at least unattended)
ladder, which reminds me
now, in autumn, of the discarded workers'
toolbox Thoreau sighted by the track.
Something has crept into our lives
and crept back out again.
I sense its measure; I sense it *in* measure,
a creature of proportions
and frail in that, as we (or I) am frail.
It slips into the burning orchard
and back out again; it rustles the long
green stems of that field of hands.
I do not know its name. If I knew its
name, I could call to it, call it
down or up. I perceive, then, it may
be a mercy I do not, cannot
know its name, because I cannot therefore
summon to myself all that lies
beyond myself, that is larger than myself.

Our lives are tangent: to each others'
and to larger forces:
at almost infinitesimal points they touch.
A groundsman shaves new growth
from my yew hedge,
and I watch him. Later, I pay him.
As far as Heraclitean fire goes
he is, at middle age, a handsome man,
at least until

he removes his hat. His skull
is bare and ugly. Once, he came to my
house on a motorcycle
with a woman riding shotgun,
to pick up a check; it was a beautiful
portrait of a midsummer day
moving rapidly into the dwindling cone.

About love, I came to it
late in life and am not sorry,
I mean it is better late than not at all
(as the saying goes),
even unrequited. In the marriage plot
of faith, I drew the Hanged Man.
I suffer him as I suffer Christ.
I keep the walls of my house bare
that he might stretch his form upon them
and I might know him
by his shadow. If he is Christ
then the vision opens again, into another:
place your hands into my wounds,
the eye, the neck abraded.
If the rope hangs from the pear tree
then is the rope on fire.
If I reach for it, is it to cut him down
or to touch his suspended inconsequence
which is my inconsequence.

In Warren's poem, it is the stridor
and the snow that follow the woodsman
from that rude Golgotha
into the exile one life constitutes:
the three made one in a cold death.
I reach for that rope
with a hand of Christ, with a hand of fire
and am handed, in return,

a pear, hard, not quite ripe, misshapen
in the stony-sweet way of pears.
I hold it against my cheek: it is cold,
a detached star dreaming
that it might understand love,
all that which can only be accepted.
If there is a choice in this
then I am deaf to it, dumb, false witness
to what might succor exigence.
Place your hand in my wounds.
Thomas's penance—for his unbelief,
for avoiding the company of his brethren
on the road to Emmaus—
was this precisely, contact, touch,
the member's brief immersion
in that purifying flame. Suffer me, Lord.

As Flesh Made New Through Burning

The gentle tremor that has begun now in my left hand, between thumb and forefinger,

is not history. Its seed lies buried deep in sleep, in the neurochemistry of sleep

which traces its faint salt patterns on the stone of my soul. Stone of my soul,

the formal world is alive with the drained pool's bracketing moss,

with insect life, with the toadflax and orpine, those useful entities that remind us

how much of a wall the heart may come to conduct, to encompass

and consume. I think of the tremor in my hand as a gentle song, a new hymn

my body has begun. There's a single cookfire on the open plain; a single eye tends it—

childhood and childhood's memories of childhood, inspiraling. The tremor,

the hymn in the hand knows nothing of either fire or eye and does not care. Song

has no compassion because through song compassion is woven

from disparate threads. My home was a wall, for a little while; I suckled there,

I brought the hand out of its glass case in the moonlight. *I will give thee*

the treasures of darkness, I read as the palm spasmed, slow gimel of praise

at 36,000 feet. And the stray stone takes its due place in the wall, to mete

out possession or else keep graves from spilling into the paths of the living. I feel

the cold wattle of roots. *Break me*, I want to whisper, while beside me

immigrant children compare chipped glyphs in the flickering curvature.

They have tasted a small dream and found it good. To worship the punishment

is banal except when it demands antiphon, response. The eye that tends the campfire

demands a siege, but I am answering the tremor in my hand

with the smallest possible service my damaged vocal cords can muster.

Sleep moves within us like another music I never clearly hear. My house is dark

and tomorrow we separate the lambs from the ewes. I have even learned

to take some pleasure in their crying. Perhaps no sin is greater than this severance.

The Completion of Shadows

Oh friends I am a prison to all that lies within me.
It burns the way phosphorus burns. It bears the raven's flag
into the ragged country called by its natives Los Arpas.
There I saw butterflies clustering at the torn throat

of the fallen antelope which came to me later
in a dream, and nourished me also with its flesh.
In the bellows of my chest a golden chant was brewing
like a cloud caught in a beautiful woman's jewelry.

And death what would you drink I asked of the body
and its innumerable spirits. *And death what would you ride*
I called into the red stable where I kept my love
among the blue wheat of the church's gapped treasures.

I was offered a living sprig from the temple gate
and asked to plant it wherever I called
home—now I call home the place where the living sprig
tattoos the earth. I drink from it, as a sparrow

from the glistening rock. There was an emperor, once,
in the Book of the Martyrs; I returned his gaze.
And I wore a strip of cloth around my biceps
when I was a young man, for the sake of the beautiful—

dawn stripped it from me. Now I see with the eyes of bread.
And death answers *I am afraid, I am so afraid,*
my little one. Don't be frightened, I say, leading death
into his narrow cell. I sing death a lullaby

amid the brightening bones, knowing that when death
wakes he will recall his true love and leave me here,
even as death's guards pursue. I who also am
a son of David, I who with lilac fletched my lover's scar.

My Beast Made of Gold Is My Vocation

My beast made of gold is my vocation; it walks with me
and makes a peaceable sound. It has no wings and it has no clay.
I never touch it, if I can help it—though sometimes, knocked
roughly, I brush it by accident. That is when the pain comes
and the great poems cover their famished faces. Which is the true
prison: the church, the garden, the body, or the mind?
My beast doesn't answer, but I detect a slight modulation
in its earthy hum. I cannot leave it and it, evidently, will
not leave me. I wish I had a cord with which to bind it up. Bless
the rain, which washes the eye clear and remembers nothing
but what we have discarded in the skies. It wraps my golden beast
in its wet hands. I want to return the earth's broad phylacteries,
which it left in my care. This is the furthest I will get from love
and love's children, adrift in the blue-eyed grass. My beast
prepares a place for me. It is not the place I wanted, but
I recognize myself in its contagious mysteries. *Oh beast surrender*
I call into the night's tight coin. It remains beside me, unblinking.
It is a beast, and I am a man. Together we make our worship.

Metobelus

And so in the third of the great dreams I am afflicted with leprosy: snow-flesh, salt-flesh, sugar-flesh, semen-flesh. Frangible and inconvenient.

In the first of the great dreams, I am waiting: senselessly, eternally. In traffic. In the anteroom of a doctor's office. In the hollow square, waiting for the singing to begin.

In the second of the great dreams there is blood: spilt blood, quantities of it. I am there and I must have committed the crime, although I have no memory of it. Or I am there and the perpetrator is, must be, nearby: I must hide. Or I am there in advance of some vaguer violence the dream gallops toward, with me inside it.

In the third of the great dreams, *nightflesh*. I wonder distractedly whether I glow in the dark. Parts of me evanesce—a finger, scooped-out hollow of a shin. The teeth and nails also, and the hair. The hair even in waking life, a marriage one wakes into: the quickening matrix, little factories sloughing off their shadow-speech.

In the fourth of the great dreams, a river—wide, muddy, swift—and beneath its surface, something sharp I can't see: only the terrifying burl in the current. Into which I am about to be hurled, by chance or circumstance within each night's logic.

Inside the cavern a figure is taking shape, *almost* luminous—maybe I imagine it, or perceive it with some faculty other than sight. It is neither welcome nor dismaying. I've lost one or both of my hands, my feet, my arms and legs.

If you remain very still you can understand the effects your life has on the lives of others. A glowing presence where the body used to stand, surrounded by water.

In that mountain town we walked among the aeolian harps, books we couldn't open. The body dreams of being blown *through*. That music, otherworldly.

The leprous body, then, as stigma, micropyle. The grains wedging deep into the plasma, and viral—if you like, a scientific fiction. Not nacreous: the scintillations of consciousness merely deflect. What from whom? Whom from what?

Flesh *vs.* anti-flesh. The lip stubbornly insists: on the vireo, the fricative, the ripening pear. As if from vaster distances, stars forming like nightfruit.

What remains of the body after the burning is not the heart, but the larynx. Vitrified and recollected.

Baptism—*for the remission of sins* the body reasons, epiphytic, held captive by the mind.

And so in the third of the great dreams the body comes away from the body, within the intelligence. You can't really make a scroll of it. You are merely an observer.

But this is now the seventh dream, in which it is you who stumbles through the ashes, you who reaches down to pick the body up—and it burns you. It burns like dry ice, the scars streaking instantly from your fingertips to your palm. You want to drop it, but you can't. It burns and you hold onto it. It burns into your waking self like an ester, an abscess, a vigil. —*Inflorescence.* Contagious, a cruciform tongue.

Acknowledgments

Many thanks to the editors of the following journals in which these poems originally appeared, some in earlier versions:

American Poetry Review: "Small Song (for Edith Stein)"
Bennington Review: "Neither Winter nor a Golden Dust"
Boulevard: "Ascension Day"
Cincinnati Review: "Common Prayer" and "My Beast Made of Gold Is My Vocation"
Colorado Review: "Like a Fire from Which Sparks Emitted Do Fly Upward"
Crazyhorse: "Candleweb, Thaw" and "Map / (after Jasper Johns)"
Denver Quarterly: "Anniversary"
Harvard Review online: "Untitled (Drone Poem)"
Image: "Fishguard Harbour"
Indiana Review: "On Setting Myself on Fire" and "The Prescriptivist"
Iowa Review: "Cancer Poem"
Kenyon Review: "Fox-Breath / (Para-Chantry)"
New American Writing: "On the Seventh Anniversary of the U.S. Invasion of Afghanistan"
New England Review: "Chipping Campden," "Their Faces Shall Be as Flames,"
    and "What David Taught, & Where He Taught It"
Ninth Letter: "Eight Short Films about Architecture" and "In Memory of Domestic Life"
Poetry Northwest: "Convocation (Psaltery)" and "The Doubled Organs"
Quarterly West: "The Fear Was in the Northeast"
Seneca Review: "Metobelus"
Shenandoah: "White Peaches"
Virginia Quarterly Review: "As Flesh Made New Through Burning"
Yale Review: "The Completion of Shadows" and "To the Embalmers"

"On the Seventh Anniversary of the U.S. Invasion of Afghanistan" was reprinted in *Haydens Ferry Review* and in *Postmodern American Poetry*, 2nd edition, edited by Paul Hoover (W. W. Norton, 2013). "The Fear Was in the Northeast" appeared on the *Verse Daily* website, September 22, 2009. "Anniversary" was reprinted in *Making Poems*, edited by Todd Davis and Erin Murphy (State University of New York Press, 2010). "Common Prayer" was reprinted in *The Poet's Quest for God: 21st Century Poems of Faith, Doubt and Wonder*, edited by Oliver Brennan and Todd Swift, et al. (Eyewear Publishing, 2016).

"Their Faces Shall Be as Flames" (which takes its title from Isaiah 13:8) also appeared in *Harper's* magazine; in *The Best American Poetry 2010,* edited by Amy Gerstler and David Lehman; and in *If Bees Are Few: A Hive of Bee Poems,* edited by James P. Lenfestey (University of Minnesota Press, 2016).

"Anniversary" is for Peter Streckfus, "Common Prayer" for and after Geri Doran, "Metobelus" for and after Peter O'Leary, and "Poem in Which I Pretend You Are Still Alive" I and II for Jennifer MacKenzie. "The Grievers" was written in memory of Slava Yastremski, at his funeral.

"The Completion of Shadows" takes its title from a phrase by the fifth-century hymn writer St. Ephrem the Syrian; the source of this book's epigraph is Sebastian Brock's "Notes to Section II of the Commentary on Genesis," published in *St. Ephrem the Syrian: Hymns on Paradise* (St. Vladimir's Seminary Press, 1997; 226–27).

St. Wenog is one of those pre-Congregation (fifth- or sixth-century) Welsh saints "of whose works nothing is known," as one calendar quaintly puts it.

"Do something to it. Do / something else to it" in "Map" quotes Jasper Johns via John Yau's *A Thing Among Things: The Art of Jasper Johns* (DAP/Distributed Art Publishers, 2008).

The Robert Penn Warren poem alluded to in "Ascension Day" is, of course, *Audubon: A Vision* (Random House, 1969).

Gratitude also to the Tyrone Guthrie Centre, the Lannan Foundation, the MacDowell Colony, and the Corporation of Yaddo, and to Rachel Galvin, Ilya Kaminsky, Tyler Meier, Dana Levin, Karla Kelsey, John Gallaher, Joshua Corey, Victoria Chang, Shane McCrae, John Cross, Harold Schweizer, and Tim Lilburn, all of whom read earlier versions of this manuscript.

Other Books from Tupelo Press

Silver Road: Essays, Maps & Calligraphies (memoir), Kazim Ali

A Certain Roughness in Their Syntax (poems), Jorge Aulicino,
    translated by Judith Filc

Another English: Anglophone Poems from Around the World (anthology),
    edited by Catherine Barnett and Tiphanie Yanique

gentlessness (poems), Dan Beachy-Quick

Personal Science (poems), Lillian-Yvonne Bertram

Everything Broken Up Dances (poems), James Byrne

One Hundred Hungers (poems), Lauren Camp

Almost Human (poems), Thomas Centolella

Land of Fire (poems), Mario Chard

Gossip and Metaphysics: Russian Modernist Poetry and Prose (anthology),
    edited by Katie Farris, Ilya Kaminsky, and Valzhyna Mort

Entwined: Three Lyric Sequences (poems), Carol Frost

Poverty Creek Journal (memoir), Thomas Gardner

Leprosarium (poems), Lise Goett

My Immaculate Assassin (novel), David Huddle

Dancing in Odessa (poems), Ilya Kaminsky

A God in the House: Poets Talk About Faith (interviews),
    edited by Ilya Kaminsky and Katherine Towler

Third Voice (poems), Ruth Ellen Kocher

A Camouflage of Specimens and Garments (poems), Jennifer Militello

The Cowherd's Son (poems), Rajiv Mohabir

After Urgency (poems), Rusty Morrison

Canto General (poems), Pablo Neruda, translated by Mariela Griffor and Jeffrey Levine

The Life Beside This One (poems), Lawrence Raab

Intimate: An American Family Photo Album (hybrid memoir), Paisley Rekdal

The Book of Stones and Angels (poems), Harold Schweizer

Good Bones (poems), Maggie Smith

Swallowing the Sea (essays), Lee Upton

Legends of the Slow Explosion: Eleven Modern Lives (essays), Baron Wormser

Ordinary Misfortunes (poems), Emily Jungmin Yoon

See our complete list at www.tupelopress.org